MY COLLEGE: MY NATION

by Adewale Adewusi (a.k.a I'm for Christ)

PRESENTED TO:

....

BY:

....

DATE:

....

Published by I'm for Christ Group of Companies.

ISBN: 978-0-9988794-2-0

Printed in the United States.

"I've found out that leadership is something you grow into naturally by just doing the best work you can; in the areas you can." President José Luis Cruz.

"I know of no single formula for success, but over the years I have observed that some attributes of leadership are universal and are often about finding ways of encouraging people to combine their efforts, their talents, their insights, their enthusiasm and their inspiration to work together." Queen Elizabeth II.

"Leadership is about making others better as a result of your presence and making sure that impacts lasts in your absence." Sheryl Sandberg COO of Facebook.

"Make a difference in this world…; be that change you wish to see." Professor Elisabeth Ostler.

"Management is doing things right; leadership is doing the right things." Peter F. Drucker.

"Men make history and not the other way around. In periods where there is no leadership, society stands still. Progress occurs when courageous, skillful leaders seize the opportunity to change things for the better." Harry S. Truman.

ACKNOWLEDGEMENT

I render thanks and adoration unto the Most-high God for giving me the strength and wisdom to write this book. Praise the Lord!

APPRECIATION

Much gratitude to all the staff and faculty members of Lehman College for their great work and support for all students; to emphasize a phrase from few of them – thanks to Mr. Miguel Pacheco (Admission Advisor) for his courageous advice to me during my enrollment period (fall 2015), he said, "the ball is in your court, just keep kicking it…" meaning that; I should not be discouraged but keep pressing forward until I achieve my goal. And my Professor in English 111 – Spring 2017, her advice to the class prior to the end of the semester, "your word matters… be that change you wish to see…" Professor Elisabeth Ostler.

As well as my fellow student leaders – The SGA officers; President Victoria Antonetti, V.P Erick J. Peguero and all others, and finally my mentors at the Leadership class – Muhammed and Leonora (Introduction – Spring 2017), and Erick J. Peguero and Sahir (Advance – Spring 2018).

A man's achievement is not only by his effort, but it is a team work.

Thanks, and God bless you all!

Adewale Adewusi
Men's soccer team #14.

DEDICATION

I dedicate this book – "My College: My Nation" to the honor of Lehman College's third president: Dr. José Luis Cruz, and to the celebration of its 50th Anniversary of **L**eading **E**very **H**uman to the **M**ost **A**ttainable heights in our **N**ation!

I hereby declare a permission for the reprinting of this book to my great college – Lehman College (CUNY) for the benefits of my fellow students.

Congratulations to President José Luis Cruz!

Your effort, achievement, leadership, voice, love, sympathy, and your goals has foster a great leadership experience in many students and have brought knowledgeable blessings to our lives and nation.

It is of a surety that the greatest courage to achieve a goal is by taking the first step today with the input of your hard work:

> "90 by 30… the end game may be in 2030 but the journey to 90 thousand starts today; it requires deliberate intentional action today." President José Luis Cruz, Ph.D.

"For us; advancing the mission of HigherEd is not just something we do, is not something we say; it's something we live." Dr. Rima Brusi, Ph.D.

"He is not just an excellent president; he's a great leader, a leader who cares." Honorable Williams C. Thompson, Jr. Chairperson, Board of Trustees, The City University of New York.

CONTENT

Chapter 1

THE ROLE OF A GOOD AND EFFECTIVE LEADER

Who is a leader?

According to the dictionary meaning; a leader is a person who guides others in achieving a goal.

A leader can also be known as a person who leads others to fulfil a certain task; a leader can be a president, manager, professor, director, and likewise a parent.

Leadership is about learning, listening, leading, lecturing, launching, and lending. So therefore, for a person to be a good leader; he or she must learn from others, listen to other's advice, willing to guide others, able to teach others, develop new goals and strategies of improvement in his work, and finally, happy to share his ideas and experience with others.

At various moments in one's lifespan, a person will be expected to play the role of a leader; either by establishing his own company, become the manager of an organization, supervising employees, etc., the role of being a leader, such as sharing of experience, guiding others to achieve a goal, or setting a goal for your own company, will eventually demand your leadership skills. That is why you must learn to become a leader!

While I was taking my leadership class, I got an understanding about leaders which states that:

A leader is a person who has a desire to fulfil his goal; lifting his company to a greater height, but for the fact that you can't achieve it all alone, which means that you have people around you – working together with you, then, you must LEAD.

L – Learning about those around you; understanding the skills of individual.

E – Establish your ideas; appointing task to each person according to his or her skills.

A – Achieve your goal, and finally,

D – Dream for more.

Another instance is a soccer coach:

A coach is a leader who has a great desire for his team to win the trophy; but despite such desire, he cannot get on the field to fulfill that goal. He must LEAD:

L – Look for fit and talented players.

E – Emphasize his desire of winning the trophy.

A – Appoint each player to his best position to achieve his goal, and finally,

D – he Dreams for more.

Those are the roles of a good and effective leader, you need to:

Learn them,

Exercise them,

Achieve your goals,

And you also **D**ream for more!

There is no one that cannot be a leader; there is no one that is too young to lead – anyone can be a leader, and likewise leadership is not about gender, it is about your listening skills, experience, diversity (working with different people), being reliable, and laying down a good example that others may learn from your practical form of leadership.

"Leadership is about the hard work. By really doing the best that you can in any moment in your life to advance the causes that you are passionate about, will naturally lead to opportunities that will provide you a bigger platform to do more of that and to do it better." President José Luis Cruz, Ph.D.

"President Cruz has become inspiration for the student body through his tireless work on behalf of Lehman college and the Bronx… he has shown that a true leader surmounts each new challenge. He has spent his time at Lehman listening, learning strengths and weaknesses, and offering new ideas; he has been collaborating with all departments and organizations to improve our college, while planning new ways to support new growth at Lehman based on his conversation with faculty, staff and students." Victoria Antonetti, President, SGA (2017/18).

NOTE

Chapter 2

"90 by 30"

President José Luis Cruz

Dr. José Luis Cruz was born in Puerto Rico, had his bachelor's degree in Electrical engineering from the University of Puerto Rico, and his Doctorate degree from Georgia Institute of Technology, married to Dr. Rima Brusi, and blessed with five children.

He started his leadership journey from 7th grade when his fellow students voted him as the president of the student council. His leadership positions as always been in a form of gift presentation to him. After exercising his usual hard work, integrity, and responsibilities, his co-workers had no choice but to present him his next available opportunity – advancing his leadership role. Right from the 7th grade as the student council president, served as a faculty member at the University of Puerto Rico; and later recommended by colleagues to be the Chair of the department of Electrical and Computer Engineering, became a Dean of Academic Affairs, Vice President of Student Affairs, served in a research and advocacy organization as the Vice President of HigherEd Policy and Practice (The Educational Trust, Washington D.C), Provost of California State University (Fullerton), and eventually, his hard works in those leadership roles at various organization presented him this opportunity to be the President of Lehman college – a college of great leaders, and ranked as 4th in the nation; lifting low income students into the middle class and beyond. A college that is attributed with his devotion to providing opportunities for its students – leading every human to the most attainable heights in our nation.

President Cruz's compassion, integrity, and hard work has resulted him with his various leadership positions. He stated, "not necessarily aspiring to be the leader, but others thought that he works hard, and he gets things done…" he realized that a leadership role is not just about having anxiety of a leadership position, but it is about your faithfulness and hard work at your present position or leadership role.

While speaking to the leadership class of Spring 2018, he advised the students, “pay attention to those that are seeing you more than you are seeing yourself.” In most of his leadership positions, after being encouraged to go for a leadership role, he sometimes felt not seeing himself in that position, but he eventually gave it a try, and enjoyed his services; which also presented him another leadership opportunity as he journeyed through to becoming the President of Lehman College – CUNY.

“… now I have the great privilege of trying to articulate the vision for the college and ensuring that we are the best we can be for you the students, for the Bronx and for New York city.” President José Luis Cruz.

Our President has discovered and revealed the future apparel that fits our economy; most especially the Bronx. His love and care for the younger generations has driven him thinking, working, learning, and planning how he can best impact the lives of the underserved.

The problem has been revealed:

The number of low-income earners is increasing because they have not been able to achieve their bachelor’s degree and beyond.

The benefit has been announced:

“If our Bronx wrestling’s age 25 and older who today have at least a high school diploma earn a bachelor’s degree, their fortunes and those of the borough would be vastly different; generating an additional $6 billion in annual income and $2.8 billion in tax revenues.” President José Luis Cruz.

This benefit will not only improve the life style of individuals; transferring them out of poverty, but it will also yield to a greater GDP!

The solution has been declared:

"90 by 30"! This goal is to increase from 45,000 to 90,000; the number of degrees and high-quality credentials that Lehman students will earn by the year 2030.

About Herbert H. Lehman; "A leader who believe that an educated generation was the true hope; not only of a free American but of a free world." President José Luis Cruz.

The work must be done:

It is definite that these benefits will not only impact the Bronx residence alone but will also cause an increase in our nation's economy – so therefore, the work must be done.

How can this goal be achieved? How can you participate in its fulfillment? As a student leader; what role can you play for the success of this goal?

With witnesses of high intellect present at the convocation and inauguration of President Cruz on the 27th of September 2017; testifying of his achievements and incredibility, it is assured that "90 by 30" can also be achieved; but it takes a "deliberate intentional action today." President José Luis Cruz.

"He is not just an excellent president; he's a great leader, a leader who cares." Honorable Williams C. Thompson, Jr. Chairperson, Board of Trustees, The City University of New York.

"For us; advancing the mission of HigherEd is not just something we do, is not something we say; it's something we live." Dr. Rima Brusi, Ph.D.

"He has devoted the passions and energies of his academic life; armed with a king organizational mind; he has produced agendas, plans, strategies, gages, and assessments to prove his case… He is simply convinced that there is no true excellence without diversity and access." Antonio Garcia Padilla, LL.M. Former President, University of Puerto Rico.

"President Cruz has become inspiration for the student body through his tireless work on behalf of Lehman college and the Bronx… he has shown that a true leader surmounts each new challenge. He has spent his time at Lehman listening, learning strengths and weaknesses, and offering new ideas; he has been collaborating with all departments and organizations to improve our college, while planning new ways to support new growth at Lehman based on his conversation with faculty, staff and students." Victoria Antonetti, President, SGA (2017/18).

Our President has created a task for us; revealing his great goal, which was inspired by his desire and love for students, HigherEd, and the nation in general, because the increase in the numbers of people with a college degree will not only impact their own lives alone, but indirectly cause great improvement in the nation's economy. According to President Cruz, he stated, "90 by 30 is meant to be a catalyst for urgent action; for the urgent action required to create the conditions whereby the promise of prosperity of a resurgent Bronx is within the reach of all those who seek to reach their full potential."

My fellow leaders; this is a goal before us, and as leaders, we have a duty to exercise our support of this goal. Your leadership is needed! Your skills, ideas, and your time; your role as a leader is needed.

As this goal is being achieved; as leaders, let's also make sure that 90% of those students earn their leadership skills, experience, and certificate. Even though, by the fulfillment of our president's goal – "90 by 30", we would have graduated, but let's develop a unique dream, idea, or social club, that will exist to attract students to become members to continue in fulfilling the mission of such club – supporting "90 by 30". In addition to varieties of clubs on campus;

LEAD can also be a good example – a group of volunteers – leaders that call student's awareness to the leadership training and assist them to register for the class – LEAD – Leadership, Efficiency, Awareness, Developers.

Finally, according to President Cruz, "… the end game may be in 2030 but the journey to 90 thousand starts today; it requires deliberate intentional action today." Let us arise in our level of creativity and ideas, and let's sit down to plan what to do to support the achievement of "90 by 30" because our leadership is needed!

"I've found out that leadership is something you grow into naturally by just doing the best work you can; in the areas you can." President José Luis Cruz, Ph.D.

AGENDA

1. What are your ideas?

2. What can we do for the accomplishment of “90 by 30”?

3. As a student; what can Lehman college do to encourage other students to enroll at Lehman college?

Chapter 3

YOUR LEADERSHIP IS NEEDED

Who is a leader but a vision-driven person, a goal-creator, skill-developer, talent-encourager. A leader! Who is a leader? Is he or she the BOSS? only **B**othering **O**ver **S**uccess without **S**uffering (always avoiding the difficulties encountered in the process of achieving a goal). Who is a leader? A leader is a goal-burden bearer; he participates in the struggles, challenges, duties and works – he is a member of the team!

Who is a leader but a co-laborer, a good-example to others, time-conscious, duty-focused, goal-driven, team-encourager, and dream-achiever; a leader is an inspirator!

Who is a LEADER? A **L**istener, **E**ffective worker, exercises good **A**ttitude, skill **D**eveloper, goal **E**stablisher, and a **R**ewarder – encouraging his team members to work more efficiently.

To be a LEADER also means: **L**earning more about the skills you already own, putting them into **E**ffect, **A**llocating more skills by learning from others, **D**evelop other people to be great leaders like you, **E**xercising your leadership skills before them, and finally, you **R**ender them your support to be greater leaders than you are!

One of the most valuable commodity of a leader is his action; that is, **a**ttitude, **c**ourage, **t**eamwork, **i**ntegrity, **o**bjective (set goal), and **n**urture (caring and encouragement of growth). And that is because people are watching you. As President Cruz stated, "not necessarily aspiring to be the leader, but others thought that he works hard, and he gets things done…" despite he was not eager to leave his leadership position, being devoted to how he can make the organization a better one; his demonstrated action have made people to offer him a greater leadership opportunity compared to his present position. So therefore, as a leader, you need to exercise a good action: Attitude, Courage, Teamwork, Integrity, Objective, and Nurture, so that your good works will be an evidence to others, for them to recommend you for better opportunities.

Your commitment, dream, expectations, plans, and finally, the decisions you make; all of these are necessary in your leadership role.

A leader has a potential that drives those around him to dream bigger and to PURSUE; **P**lanning, **U**rgency, **R**epeating; never to give up if failed, **S**earching for the right people to work with, **U**nderstanding each other, and finally, **E**xhibit your fulfilled goals.

"A dream with a day becomes a goal" Erick J. Peguero (V.P LCSGA).

Congratulations to our previous and current graduating leaders!

As titled, "Your leadership is needed"

First and foremost, I am happy to announce to you that you are a special leader and your role is a crucial one.

Secondly, I am here to encourage you to use your leadership and personal skills for the benefit and improvement of our college, as well as our fellow students out there.

Finally, in honor and support to our president's great goal, "90 by 30"! As this goal is being fulfilled, as leaders, we also need to encourage our fellow students to know about the importance of this free-leadership training and assist them to register for the class, because Lehman College is a great college with great leaders, and every Lehman student also need to have that leadership skill before they graduate.

I would also like to encourage you to listen to an online video titled, "The Role of a Good and Effective Leader" by Adewale Adewusi.

Leadership is revealing who you are; that is, sharing your experience in form of advising and teaching others to encourage them to be better leaders with their already owned skills and talents.

"This leadership program has allowed me to realize the importance of articulating our vision to others, while being open-minded enough to give the opportunity for them to join our idea as a shared-vision." Ibrahim Souare.

"You matter, your voice matters… make a difference in this world…; be that change you wish to see." Professor Elisabeth Ostler.

"Being a part of the Herbert H. Lehman leadership program helped me redefine what being a leader means and allowed me to foster both the sense of confidence and determination needed to be an advocate for change." Shabel Castro.

Exploring your leadership abilities while still a student prepares you fit for a more-demanding role that you might be given at your desired job after graduation.

"The leadership program taught me that a true leader is moved by the act of love towards humanity and devoted for the justice and needs of others." Guillermo Jesus Escano.

"I've found out that leadership is something you grow into naturally by just doing the best work you can; in the areas you can." President José Luis Cruz.

A student is a future leader; awaited by great positions such as president, governor, minister, director, manager, provost, counselor, chair-person, dean, and so on, but it takes leadership skills to attain them and function effectively.

NOTE

Chapter 4

MY COLLEGE: MY NATION

Education brings diversification; it helps one to be able to work with others. It also helps one to gain the benefits of learning from others; understanding that there are somethings you don't know!

EDUCATION:

To be educated **E**ncourages a person to learn more, makes one **D**edicated to how to develop a solution for people's need, gain more **U**nderstanding about the world in general, gives one **C**aution on how to do things, **A**llocate his resources efficiently, gives her the ability to **T**each others, **I**nspire them, **O**bserve them, and **N**urture them properly.

"Education is the most powerful weapon which you can use to change the world." Nelson Mandela.

"There is no question that educational attainment opens the doors to economic and social mobility, not just for students, but also for their families" President Ruben Diaz, Jr. (Bronx Borough).

Education is for all,

College is for all,

Opportunities are for all,

And Lehman college is there for all! – Leading Every Human to the Most Attainable heights in our Nation!

"A college that notwithstanding the growth of its professional programs, remains fiercely committed to extending the benefits of a liberal education to all of its students regardless of the course of study they choose to pursue." President José Luis Cruz.

I love Lehman College, and it's a pride for me to be part of such a great college; established, driven, and run by great leaders.

"Here at Lehman, we are lucky to be surrounded by thoughtful determined leaders across the campus." Victoria Antonetti, President, SGA (2017/18).

A college established with the benefits of improvement and development of its students: endowed with great opportunities, wonderful facilities, career services, scholarship programs, leadership programs, and much more. A college recognized for propelling low-income students into the middle class – preparing every human; regardless of their color or race, for excellency in a competitive world.

According to Mr. Vincent Prohaska, Ph.D. Professor, Psychology & Chair, Executive Committee of General Faculty, "our college has maintained the same fundamental mission since its founding; to be a college that matters, to be a college where education is a life changing phelonion, to be a college where the degrees our students earn pave road towards solid futures in career trajectories, to be a college whose graduates can provide even greater possibilities for their children, to be a college that enriches the Bronx. Lehman college is a remarkable institution that deserves remarkable leaders."

A place of a credibility of peace among the students and staff members in general!

This world can be a better place for all humanity to live together if only we can exercise similar love and care that President Cruz, Mr. José Magdaleno – Vice President of Student Affairs, professors (Elisabeth Ostler, John-Paul A. etc.), other staffs and faculty members, Mr. Michael Sullivan (Director of Campus Life), Ms. Suzette Ramsundar (Associate Director, Campus Life & Coordinator H.H.L. Center For Student Leadership Development), student mentors, and members of SGA, etc. these people were not only focused on their goal of attending or working in a college, and despite that most of them never meet until now at this institution, they all manifested their love and care which foster a great impact in my life as a student, as well as my fellow students.

These great impacts in the lives of students; which also yielded to an economy improvement – “raising students of low-income into the middle class and beyond,” couldn’t have been a reality if not for the following:

1. Humility:

While I was taking my introduction to leadership class in Spring 2017, President Crus regarded not the numbers of student in attendance, which were less than 20, but he was humble enough to come and address us; showing us the good example of a leader. During his speech, he said, “I go around; visiting each group, listening to their ideas, and then work on them to the improvement of the college and benefit of the students.” The effect of humility brings progress, efficiency, and effectiveness to our college, as well as the society and our nation.

2. Care:

Our school leaders (professors, advisors, members of the career services, etc.) teach and helps students to be better leaders in our world, and the student directors; Mr. Michael Sullivan, and Ms. Suzette Ramsundar, they train students to become great leaders – aiding them to recognize and exercise their leadership skills. Some of these students have become members of the Student Government Association: seeking better opportunities for the students, while some started clubs and develop various programs to meet the needs of their fellow students. Clubs such as Intervarsity and SEEK Christian fellowship, Music club, ALPHA, NASBA, Muslim fellowship, DREAM team, and lots more, including the Lehman college Food Bank; which has been of great benefit to me as a student! Going to the food pantry is like going to shop at the supermarket for free; making selection among varieties of foods available. It helps students spend less money on food, spend less hours on working, and spend more hours on our studies – which is our prioritized purpose of being in college and qualifies us as student – studies! You **S**earch for new knowledge, **T**est what you've learnt (practice), **U**nderstand the world around you, **D**evelop new ideas to improve the lives of those around you, **I**ntroduce your acquired knowledge to others, **E**ncourage others to be well educated, and finally, you **S**how them the available resources to be a successful student.

The role of leadership continues to extend because there are always student leaders on campus; even after many have graduated. What a great impact through the act of love and caring for others!

"To this day, I am of the mind that my teacher's sharp focus and open heart, helped shaped the trajectory of my life; a life that has benefited from, and been dedicated to the idea promulgated by Horace Mann, that education beyond all other devices of human origin is the great equalizer of the condition of men; the balance wheel of the social machinery." President José Luis Cruz.

The role of a teacher; teaching, guiding, leading, encouraging, caring, as well as correcting student's wrong actions, is one that strengthens students to be their best and become a better teacher for the future students.

"The leadership program taught me that a true leader is moved by the act of love towards humanity and devoted for the justice and needs of others." Guillermo Jesus Escano.

3. Leadership:

Successes in Lehman College derived from the manifestation of leadership attributes and qualifications; "A leader is a person who desire to fulfil his goal, but for the fact that you have people working with you; which means that you can't achieve it all alone, then, you must LEAD…" (Chapter 1: the role of a good and effective leader). Our leaders were able to pay good attention to the ideas of others, aligned them with theirs, accomplish their desired goals, and foster more goals for the improvement of our college such as "90 by 30".

With the effect, these great leaders have manifested courageous advice to students. During my enrollment period to Lehman College in fall 2015, after I failed my entrance examination, Mr. Miguel Pacheco encouraged me, saying, “the ball is in your court; don’t stop, just keep kicking it forward.” meaning that; I should not be discouraged but keep pressing forward until I achieve my goal. He also referred me to an advisor – Mr. Konstantinos Filis (Program Specialist, ADP), who eventually advised me to take an extra class as a better preparation for the entrance exam, of which I took a writing class with Professor Steve Dowling, and he also encourage me to make use of an online math tutorial called Khan Academy to avoid the cost of taking the class.

4. Diversity:

“Lehman college is a mixture of so many cultures, financial backgrounds, religion, interests, stories, and more.” Victoria Antonetti, President, SGA (2017/18).

Lehman college is not just there to grant you higherEd degree, but she is also there to care for you like a mother. She has developed lots of resources for the benefits of her students, for them not to be overwhelmed in times of challenges. Scholarships, financial aid, community engagement, leadership development, and food pantry are available to all students – no worries about what to eat! Students are encouraged to work on campus to begin their engagement with the community prior to their graduation when they will be working in the ‘bigger world.’

There are variety of clubs that can fit your schedule, interest, passion, ability, skill, knowledge etc. They are all established for you!

You are highly welcome to Lehman college: the college that is always there for you, recognized for student’s success, academic improvement, and your leadership development!
Lehman college! A college of great leaders, a college of great students, and a college of future leaders! That's my College!

With these great effect of my college leaders; isn't it possible for such characteristics of humility, care (love), leadership, support, etc. to be exercised in our nation?

Of course, it is possible. And there will also be a great improvement in our nation in general. But as it is written,

> *Except the LORD build the house, they labor in vain that build it: except the LORD keep the city, the watchman wake but in vain.* Psalms 127:1,

It is expected of us as a nation to humbly return to the LORD our creator with a determined mind of total obedience to his word. It is one of the simplest reasonable understanding that man did not create himself neither did he came into existence all by himself or was "translated from a gorilla;" no, but the Most-high God created you, and you are subject to his instructions. Just as your mobile phone did not foster itself, so is every human being.

The manufacturer as programmed this device (giving it some instructions) to function in a specific way, and it has no choice but to abide with those instructions because if otherwise, the manufacturer will dismantle it and develop another one. For human; God also has the power to erase his existence (taking off his life) when he is disobedient to his instructions, but due to his great love towards his creatures; God exercises longsuffering –

> *God is not slack concerning his promises but having long suffering,* ***not willing that any should perish but that all should come to repentance.*** 2 Peter 3:9.

He expects everyone that are disobedient to his word (instructions) to repent, because if such person dies in sin (which means a disobedient to God's word) will not get to heaven, but such person will perish in hell.

In addition, when the manufacturer detects a virus on that phone, he will install an antivirus on it to remove the virus and protect the phone from damage, but if that phone does not support the antivirus software for installation; within a short period, that phone will be damaged by the virus. In relation to God and human being, we have the following illustration:

- Manufacturer – God
- Mobile phone – Human
- Virus – sin
- Antivirus – Jesus Christ; the perfect Lamb of God that takes away the sin of the world (John 1:29)!

So therefore, it is needful for everyone who are still in disobedience to the commandment of the Most-high God who has created us, to repent and turn away from such sin.

God loves each and everyone of us; regardless of our religion, nationality, race, culture, or language because he made us all. But we are expected to humble ourselves before him because God deserves our respect, our worship, and our total obedience to his command.

Thank you!

God bless you and bless our nation.

NOTE

Chapter 5

CONFIDENCE IN GIVING A SPEECH

Giving a speech or standing in front of audience has been a challenging task to many people. And probably, there might be someone in this place that doesn't like to stand in front of audience to give a presentation. But as leaders this is an important role that we must learn, because leadership role also involve presentation. As a student mentor, teacher, CEO, manager, and so on; you are expected at some time to sit your employees down and present the company's set goals to them, so that you can all work together.

It was a surprise for me when I realized that there are some students who haven't been able to participate in the leadership class because of glossophobia.

There was a course-mate of mine which I spoke to about this leadership class and its benefit, but she asked me a question that states, "how is it like? I hope I won't be asked to give a presentation in front of the class, because I don't like it."

And for her not to be discouraged or scared, I told her that even if you must give a presentation, you will be with your group-mates. Two weeks later, I was able to talk to her immediately after class and asked if she had registered for the class, but she said, "no."

Like that my course-mate, many people have not been able to embrace great opportunities because of being timid. But we need to keep on encouraging them; to let them know about the advantages of the group presentation that are held in the leadership classes, and finally, the benefits of the leadership class.

What are the benefits of attending this leadership class?

1. You gain leadership experience,
2. Leadership skills,
3. Knowledge,
4. You gain improvement on the skills you already have,
5. You will get your certificate!
6. And finally, this great experience will be reflected on your resume, of which every employer is looking forward to seeing – a leader; someone who is able to work along with others and able to lead others in achieving a goal.

Illustration about your boldness in giving a speech:

The first reason for your confidence in giving a speech is that your speech is about what you know, and you are willing to share it with your audience.

Demonstration:

A student was called on stage with her willingness to share what she has learnt from this leadership class. After she has joyfully narrated her experience, the teacher asked, "what advise can you give to those who have not participated in the leadership class?" and she replied, they can become a better leader!

Explanation:

The thing to understand about that conversation is that:

Giving a speech is like having a conversation with your friend; while the student was sharing her experience; the teacher, and her fellow students were quiet.

Now, giving a speech also takes the same format:

1. You are already familiar with what you want to talk about.

2. You are happy to share what you know.

3. Your audience are there to listen to you just like your friends would do.

4. Ask if they have any question and answer them as much as you can.

and finally,

5. You appreciate their time and attention, and you leave the stage!

That's all about giving a speech.

I hope you will exercise this easy way of giving a speech, and play your leadership role more perfectly, because leadership role requires your presentations.

NOTE

Chapter 6

STUDENT

Who is a student?

A student is a person who is committed to learning; willing to improve his knowledge on the things around him, and to increase his educational level for better opportunities in life.

The position of a student is an incomparable one, and an unavoidable bridge; it is the bridge that leads to great successes in life.

It is a bridge trafficked with lots of studies, training, unavoidable projects and assignments, leadership development, endurance, and much more; it's a bridge trafficked with a lot of teachers!

Every teacher was once a student. A student is a sub-leader, but there is no student without a teacher.

Prior to the end of the Spring 2017 semester, my English Professor presented a speech to the class; encouraging the students about our importance in this world and the impact we can make in our lives and of those around us. She said, "… you matter, your voice matters; you are currently worthy to participate in the global conversation of things that are happening in this world; so see that and do something, and make a difference in this world, make a difference in your homes, make a difference in your own life, make a difference in your world; whoever you come in contact with, be that change that you wish to see, and writing is the fundamental way you can do that; so be creative and do that…" Professor Elisabeth Ostler.

I was glad to have professor Elisabeth and many others as my professors; for their courageous advises, interactive lecturing–skills, and commitment, because a great college with great professors can with no doubt develop great students and build future leaders.

STUDENTS: We are the **S**ustaining **T**reasures that are **U**nique and **D**esigned for the **E**fficiency of our **N**ation because we are **T**eachers to the future **S**tudents!

My experience at Lehman can be titled – commitment. It is my pleasure to be part of Lehman college men's soccer team; not just the soccer team alone but Lehman college as a whole. My Coaches and professors have helped me to be a better student athlete, and also to experience a successful time management. I am a student leader, an athlete, a writer, and I am also working; all being a Lehman Student! As a student I was able to experience more of the grace of God, because looking back at those moment of attending classes, going to work, training, writing, as well as attending church activities; all within 168 hours a week, I could not but acknowledge that I was sustained by the grace of the Most-high God!

Student:

I am a student; your fellow student.

I am a student; a human being.

I am a student; taught by a professor like other students.

I am a student; a good and well-behaved student.

I am a student; an independent student, but dependent on God!

I am a student; taught by a great Teacher; A teacher from on high, a teacher come from the Most-high God, – *There was a man of the Pharisees, named Nicodemus, a ruler of the Jews: vs2, The same came to Jesus by night, and said unto him, Rabbi,* ***we know that thou art a teacher come from God: for no man can do these miracles that thou does, except God be with him*** John 3:1&2.

My teacher made me to understand that:

I am a writer, he is the author.

I am a student, he is the teacher.

I am a learner, he is the knowledge-giver, and finally,

I am an apprentice, and he is my master!

People might be scared to pick up a book that is written by an invisible person or to even obey the divine instructions written in it; but there will be more willingness to read a book, when they see or hear of their fellow human being as the 'author,' and be overwhelmed with the hope and joy to meet such person someday.

Brief illustration: The deliverance of the Israelites from the land of Egypt.

Book of Exodus 3:8-10, *... vs8, So I have come down to rescue them from the hand of the Egyptians and to bring them up out of that land into a good and spacious land, a land flowing with milk and honey the home of the Canaanites, Hittites, Amorites, Perizzites, Hivites and Jebusites. vs 9 And now the cry of the Israelites has reached me, and I have seen the way the Egyptians are oppressing them. vs10 So now, go. I am sending you to Pharaoh to bring my people the Israelites out of Egypt.* Regarding that bible passage – it was God who was going to deliver the Israelites from their bondage, but he decided to use Moses' as a means of manifestation – revealing his glorious and mighty power to deliver the Israelites from the land of Egypt.

That is who I am as an 'author.' I am a vessel; an instrument in God's hand!

This opportunity of being an 'author' was only by the grace and love of God for me; hired me as an unskilled employee and gave me the wisdom to write and publish his knowledge to all humanity. I am blessed and highly favored!

Gratitude to Our Teachers:

Our appreciation is very important towards our teachers; we cannot but to still give them a smile at every peak of our success and achievements in life. We may sometimes feel sad about those 'packages' of projects and assignments which are included with our necessary hours of study for a successful outcome on our examinations, but I believe it was all for our benefits so that we can learn to be better STUDENTS - The **S**ustaining **T**reasures that are **U**nique and **D**esigned for the **E**fficiency of our **N**ation, because we are **T**eachers to the future **S**tudents!

"To this day, I am of the mind that my teacher's sharp focus and open heart, helped shaped the trajectory of my life; a life that has benefited from, and been dedicated to the idea promulgated by Horace Mann, that education beyond all other devices of human origin is the great equalizer of the condition of men; the balance wheel of the social machinery." President José Luis Cruz.

Our teachers; right from kindergarten have helped build a bright future for us. Their courageous advice when learning seems to be too difficult, their patience when it took us a long period to recite alphabet A to Z, or understand mathematical formulas such as algebra, calculus, and so on. They have always been our second-parents in school; teaching and training us to become better leaders for future generations.

With much gratitude to all teachers; on behalf of my fellow students, I want to appreciate all your hard works and love by saying: Thank you!

Likewise, we would not but acknowledge and appreciate our lovely parents who had also showed us their love, care, support, and courage so that we can attain a greater height in educational level. Thanks to our lovely parents!

"Education is the most powerful weapon which you can use to change the world." Nelson Mandela.

Thanks to our parents that we could be educated! and thanks to our teachers for their patience in teaching us!

The Best Leadership:

Leadership is the quality of your being. Leadership is revealing who you are; that is, sharing your experience in the form of advising and teaching others to encourage them to be a better leader with their already owned skills and talents.

Leadership means; to develop what you have (skills) by working together with others; not just laying down orders without participating in the work. A leader is not a BOSS: only **B**othering **O**ver **S**uccess without **S**uffering (always avoiding the difficulties encountered in the process of achieving a goal), but he is a Listener, Exercises a good example, Acknowledges his mistake, Develop goals, Encourage others to become better leaders, and finally, Reward his co-workers for their great efforts.

While Mr. José Magdaleno (Vice President of Student Affairs) was advising the students at an event where the students get to know those in the student government association and their various roles, titled – "meet your representatives" (Spring 2018); he encourages the student's involvement in the leadership roles, stating that as students, "you have a voice and a vote."

As a student leader, you can create more opportunities for yourself and those around you. Exploring your leadership abilities while still a student, prepares you fit for your desired job after graduation, but "you are not going to be able to do that without no involvement, without no input, without no advice…" Mr. José Magdaleno.

To be a LEADER means:

Learning more about the skills you already own, putting them into **E**ffect, **A**llocating more skills by learning from others, **D**evelop other people to be great leaders like you, **E**xercising your leadership skills before them, and finally, you **R**ender them your support to be greater leaders than you are!

Leaders lead:

Lead others to become leaders, **E**ncourage them to become good leaders, **A**ssist them to become great leaders, and finally, **D**evelops more people into the leadership field.

"This leadership program has allowed me to realize the importance of articulating our vision to others, while being open-minded enough to give the opportunity for them to join our idea as a shared-vision." Ibrahim Souare.

"The leadership program taught me that a true leader is moved by the act of love towards humanity and devoted for the justice and needs of others." Guillermo Jesus Escano.

To be a student is an important choice but to be a leader is an expected quality because these present students are the future leaders: They are the **S**ustaining **T**reasures that are **U**nique and **D**esigned for the **E**fficiency of our **N**ation and to **T**each the future **S**tudents!

As students; "you have a voice and a vote," "your voice matters..." and your leadership is very important in our nation!

NOTE:

TESTIMONY: GOD IS A TREASURE FOR EVERYONE THAT BELONGS TO HIM!

My name is Adewale Adewusi. I am an immigrant from West Africa – Nigeria. I got to the United States in November 2014, started working in 2015, enrolled in college in 2016, and finally transferred to my first choice of college in 2017!

After my first semester at Globe Institute of Technology, I transferred to Lehman College (CUNY) – Spring 2017. Having the opportunity to earn a college degree without a prior down payment was a great benefit for me; so therefore, I went ahead to pursue the goal of becoming a college graduate – majoring in Business Administration with Account concentration!

The Great Intervention:

Prior to the end of Fall 2017 semester. I had a reduction of my working hours on my job, from about the range of 10 - 20 hours a week to 5 hours a week. So, I had to manage paying my rent until 30th of December, and when I realized that I can't afford the 150 dollars for the following week, I told my room owner to use my deposited payment for the first week of January and I will be moving on the 7th (with the hope that God would provide a place to move too). Luckily, on the 7th, I found my church member who permitted me to come and stay with him until the end of the month; which will be the beginning of the Spring 2018 semester.

I tried searching for a new job, but I was unable to find the one that fits my class schedule which consists of both morning, afternoon, and night classes. I had made that schedule with the hope of still having my over-night job; working as a stock-person at Dollar Tree store.

Before the end of the month of January; having learnt about the opportunities available for students who are having emergency; I went to apply for housing assistant at the office of the student affairs, and I was told to search for a place to rent before an assistance can be rendered. Unfortunately, I was unable to find a room (in a shared apartment), so I had to plead with that my church member (Mr. Emmanuel), and by God's grace and favor, he permitted me to stay until I find a room to rent and even promised to join me in the search of a room.

Prior to the beginning of the Spring semester, I had exhausted my unlimited metro card, so upon the resumption, I had to wait at the train stations until I find a help for a swipe to attend my classes as well as to return home.

The 125th street train station on the East side became my second-personal library; considering my school library as the first. Regarding access to the internet; sometimes when I feel like spending extra hours on my class assignments, I switch from the school library after its closing hours to the manageable spot beside the side walk at the train station – the 4, 5 & 6 lines on the uptown level. After connecting to the free Wi-Fi, place my laptop on my laps, have my water bottle and some cookies by my side, guard my ears with my earphones, then, I get on with my work!

Thanks be to God Almighty;

God bless America, and God bless MTA!

Finally, by the grace of God I was able to have a successful Spring 2018 semester; I made use of the food pantry at the student life building and I also got assistance from the office of student affairs with a month unlimited metro card, and two gift cards which I managed throughout the semester.

I am so grateful to the Most-high God for these opportunities! I did not drop out of college due to my challenges because my God sustained me! Hallelujah! The Lord is my treasure!

Thanks to Lehman College, Faculty members, staffs, and the student leaders.

Yours sincerely,

Adewale Adewusi

Leadership is about being a good example to others; it's about leading others – it is a path of life that consist of endurance in time of challenges, advising others to be courageous, desiring to teach others to become better leaders, encouraging those in difficulties; never to quit their dreams, rendering help for those in need, serving others, hoping for goal-achievement, improving the efforts on achieving your goal, and proving to be a good leader by your great leadership roles.

For one to exercise the best leadership role; such person must need to learn from a good leader.

About our Lord and savior Jesus Christ: a holy, sinless, and perfect image of God; appointed to die for the sin of all humanity. The great goal was set; that if achieved, all that believe on him would have the same victory over sin and gain eternal life.

1 John 3:8 *He who sins is of the devil, for the devil has sinned from the beginning. For this purpose, the Son of God was manifested, that He might destroy the works of the devil.* and John 3:16 *For God so loved the world that He gave His only begotten Son, that whoever believes in Him should not perish but have everlasting life.*

This goal was almost abolished because of the pain and challenges encountered, but he endured; laying down a good example for me. And he prayed, "*Saying, Father, if thou be willing, remove this cup from me:* ***nevertheless, not my will, but thy will be done.***" Luke 22:42. He almost quit his mission due to the suffering and difficulties, but he endured; committing himself to the perfect plan of the Heavenly Father – saying, despite my prayer and willingness to quit my mission of coming to this world (to die for the sin of all humanity), let your own will alone be done in my life: ... ***nevertheless, not my will, but thy will be done.*** " Luke 22:42.

With this great attribute of my Lord Jesus Christ; I have learnt to be courageous, and to endure all situation with total trust on the Most-high God, because he has a better plan for my life. The path to success may feel too challenging and looks so terrible, but let's maintain hope, and exercise patience; never to quit our dreams, because the painful and difficult moments will soon be over!

Advice from King Solomon:

"Start with God - the first step in learning is bowing down to God; *... Vs 8.* ***Pay close attention, friend, to what your father tells you; never forget what you learned at your mother's knee. Vs 9. Wear their counsel like flowers in your hair, like rings on your fingers."*** King Solomon (Book of Proverbs 1:7-9).

Learning to trust in the Living God, gives one a courageous confidence in times of need; enduring your situation without illegal action!

May we all continue to move from victory unto victory, testimony unto testimony until eternity, in Jesus name. Amen. *And they overcame him by the blood of the Lamb, and by the word of their testimony....* Revelations 12:11.

THANKS FOR READING, GOD BLESS!

If you have any comment; you can please send me a message on: Im4christcustomerservice@gmail.com

Thank you,

Adewale Adewusi.

References:

"2016 Lehman College Academic Convocation"
https://www.youtube.com/watch?v=IjaTzuTvmxg

"Lehman College Convocation and Inauguration 2017"
https://www.youtube.com/watch?v=x2FS52IGm3s

Tirella, Joseph. "At Inauguration, Lehman College President José Luis Cruz Announces Bold Plan to Grant 90,000 Degrees and Certificates by 2030" *http://www1.cuny.edu/mu/forum/2017/09/28/at-inauguration-lehman-college-president-jose-luis-cruz-announces-bold-plan-to-grant-90000-degrees-and-certificates-by-2030/* September 28, 2017.

www.ingramcontent.com/pod-product-compliance
Ingram Content Group UK Ltd.
Pitfield, Milton Keynes, MK11 3LW, UK
UKHW020137250726
13967UKWH00002B/711

9 780998 879420